Body Talk

In Your Genes

GENETICS AND REPRODUCTION

Steve Parker

www.raintreepublishers.co.uk
Visit our website to find out more information about **Raintree** books.

To order:
☎ Phone 44 (0) 1865 888113
▤ Send a fax to 44 (0) 1865 314091
▢ Visit the Raintree bookshop at **www.raintreepublishers.co.uk**
to browse our catalogue and order online.

First published in Great Britain by Raintree,
Halley Court, Jordan Hill, Oxford, OX2 8EJ, part
of Harcourt Education.
Raintree is a registered trademark of Harcourt
Education Ltd.

Editorial: Melanie Waldron, Rosie Gordon,
and Megan Cotugno
Design: Philippa Jenkins, Lucy Owen,
and John Walker
Illustrations: Darren Linguard and Jeff Edwards
Picture Research: Mica Brancic and
Ginny Stroud-Lewis
Production: Chloe Bloom

Originated by Dot Gradations Ltd, UK
Printed and bound in China by South China
Printing Company

10 digit ISBN: I 406 20063 8 (hardback)
13 digit ISBN: 978-1-4062-0063-8
10 09 08 07 06
10 9 8 7 6 5 4 3 2 1

10 digit ISBN 1 406 20069 7 (paperback)
13 digit ISBN 978 1 4062 0069 0
11 10 09 08 07
10 9 8 7 6 5 4 3 2 1

**British Library Cataloguing in
Publication Data**
Parker, Steve
 In your genes! : genetics and reproduction. -
(Body talk)
 1.Human genetics - Juvenile literature
2.Human reproduction
 - Juvenile literature
 I.Title
 599.9'35
A full catalogue record for this book is available
from the British Library.

Acknowledgements
The publishers would like to thank the following
for permission to reproduce photographs:

Alamy Images **pp.**18; 5, 4-5 (Visions of America);
Corbis **pp.** 6-7, 8; 21 (Luis Enrique Ascui/
Reuters), **pp.** 26-27 (Walter Smith), **p.** 36
(Bettmann), **p.** 42 (Gabe Palmer), **pp.** 14-15
(Charles O'Rear); Getty Images **pp.** 5, 15, 17, 24,
26 (Photodisc), **p.** 31 (Photonica), **pp.** 32-33
(Taxi), **p.** 41 (Stone), **pp.** 42-43 (The Image
Bank); Getty Images News **pp.** 16-17; Science
Photo Library **pp.** 14, 22; 5, 23 (TEK Image), **p.** 6
(David Scharf), **p.** 7 (Simon Fraser), **pp.** 9, 20, 28,
29 (Steve Gschmeissner), **p.** 9 (Andrew Syred),
pp. 10-11, 34 (Eye of Science), **p.** 13,
(Corbis/Digital Art), **p.** 12, (A. Barrington
Brown), **p.** 16 (Andrew Syred), **p.** 21 (Dr Paul
Andrews, University of Dundee), **p.** 25 (Du Cane
Medical Imaging LTD), **p.** 35 (Zephyr), **pp.** 37,
38 (Edelmann), **p.** 39 (Garry Watson), **p.** 40 (Dr
Najeeb Layyous), **p.** 39 (Alex Bartel); The
Advertising Archives, **p.** 24.

Cover photograph of baby reproduced with
permission of Masterfile/Pierre Tremblay.

The author and publisher would like to thank
Ann Fullick for her assistance in the preparation
of this book.

Every effort has been made to contact copyright
holders of any material reproduced in this book.
Any omissions will be rectified in subsequent
printings if notice is given to the publishers.

The paper used to print this book comes from
sustainable resources.

Disclaimer
All the Internet addresses (URLs) given in this
book were valid at the time of going to press.
However, due to the dynamic nature of the
Internet, some addresses may have changed, or
sites may have ceased to exist since publication.
While the author and publishers regret any
inconvenience this may cause readers, no
responsibility for an such changes can be
accepted by either the author or the publishers.

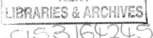
Dedicated to the memory of Lucy Owen

Contents

Any words appearing in the text in bold, **like this**, are explained in the glossary. You can also look out for them in 'Body language' at the bottom of each page.

Nobody like me!

"People say I'll look more like my mum as I grow older. I don't know if that's true. There's not much I can do about it anyway, so why worry."

Joss, aged 13, whose mother won a "Beautiful Granny Contest" at the age of 46.

Have you looked in the mirror today? Looking back at you would be a very familiar face – and a unique, one-off face. Even if you searched all over the world, there would be no one else with your looks and physical appearance.

There are plenty of human bodies to check out – more than 6,000 million worldwide. (If you said "Hi" to each one non-stop, it would take you 200 years!) But they are all different. Even the people who are most similar to each other, identical twins, are not exactly the same.

The world has billions of faces, ➤ but every one is different. This is due to the genes that people receive from their parents, life experiences they have while growing up, and also makeup, hairstyles, clothes, and hats!

Basically similar

We are all unique, yet we are all similar too. Human bodies usually have two eyes, a nose, a mouth, arms and legs, fingernails and toenails. This basic body design for people is the same everywhere. So people are different yet similar. In particular, you are more like members of your family than people you are not related to.

Deep inside

The main reason for people being basically similar, but all different as individuals, is deep inside us in our **genes**. When we understand what genes are, and how they work, we can begin to understand what makes each of us an individual.

Find out later ...

What needs 47 pairs, while you only have 23?

What is a genetic fingerprint?

Why some people have dimples, and some do not?

Instructions for life

How many genes?

The human body has about 30,000 genes. All together, they form the **human genome** – that's the name of the complete set of instructions for how the body grows and lives. All other living things have genes too. Many have more genes than us, even if they are smaller than us.

Rice plant	over 40,000
Human	about 30,000
Mouse	about 29,000
Nematode (tiny worm)	19,100
Fruit fly (below)	13,600

Imagine you are building a robot or computer. In front of you is a large table covered of bits of wire, microchips, circuit boards, screws, and other items. They are pieces of hardware; the physical bits for building what you need.

To put them together, you'll need a set of instructions, in the form of a building plan. Once the computer is assembled, it needs to be programmed with a set of working instructions too. These tell it how to carry out tasks like word processing, graphics and games.

To build a house from many parts, we use instructions. The body builds and runs itself using its own, built-in instructions, called genes. ➤

Building and running

The body needs plans and instructions too. Its building plans show it how to grow and develop from a baby to a child to an adult. Its working instructions tell it how to work and run itself day by day, as it carries out essential tasks like breathing, eating and moving. The instructions for a machine are usually on sheets of paper or a screen. Your body's instructions are inside you, and are called its **genes**. They are in the form of a chemical substance known as **DNA**.

Different types of genes

Genes don't only affect the body's outer appearance, like skin colour and adult height. They also carry instructions for how the inner parts of the body are made, like the stomach, lungs, heart, liver, kidneys ... and hundreds more.

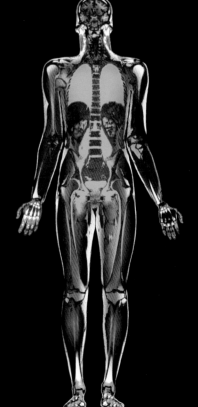

Millions of tiny skin cells form patterns of swirly ridges on our fingers, called fingerprints (below). These are controlled mostly by genes. Everyone has different fingerprints, which are often used for security identification.

Genes on or off?

Any big machine has lots of small parts working together inside. A jumbo-jet has over four million! But your human body beats this easily. It has over 50 million million. To fit them all in, each working part is **microscopic**. About 30 of them placed end to end would stretch across the dot on this "i". These micro-parts are called **cells**.

Different cells

Your body has many different kinds of cells inside. These have different shapes, sizes and jobs. Thousands of long, thin muscle cells make up your muscles. Even longer, thinner **nerve** cells form your nerves. Spider-shaped bone cells make your bones, and so on. There are over different 200 kinds of cells, forming all your body parts.

Certain cells only "switch on" the genes that they need to build the part of the body they are in charge of, like skin or hair. ▶

nerves   string-like parts that carry messages around the body as tiny pulses of electricity

Take what you need

Each of these tiny cells has the body's **genes** inside – all 30,000 of them, in the form of the chemical **DNA**. But each cell does not use them all. It uses only the ones which tell it how to do its own specialized job. So in a muscle cell, the "muscle" genes are switched on, but the rest are switched off. Likewise a skin cell has the "skin" genes turned on, but the others do not work. This gene-switching happens all over the body, in millions of different cells.

Life and death

Your genes tell each cell how to grow, what shape to become, what job to do – and when to die. **Red blood cells** (above) carry life-giving **oxygen** from your lungs to all your body parts. They all live for about the same time, three months, then they die as they are replaced by more red cells. This life span information is "programmed" into all body cells.

oxygen   gas which makes up one-fifth of air, and which the body needs
red blood cells   cells specialized to carry oxygen around the body

Size of DNA

- ✦ DNA is incredibly thin, but amazingly long.

- ✦ If half a million strands of DNA were put side by side they would measure only one millimetre across.

- ✦ If all the 46 strands of DNA in one single cell were joined end to end, they would stretch about 2 m.

- ✦ If the same was done to all the DNA in all the cells of the whole body, then the DNA would stretch from the Earth to the Sun and back more than 100 times!

Where are genes?

You might be used to following instructions which are words and pictures. Of course the **genetic** instructions are not words or pictures. They are in the form of the thread-like chemical substance called **DNA**.

There are 46 different strands of DNA inside each cell. These strands are called **chromosomes**. Each chromosome has its own share of **genes**, and between all 46, they contain 30,000 genes.

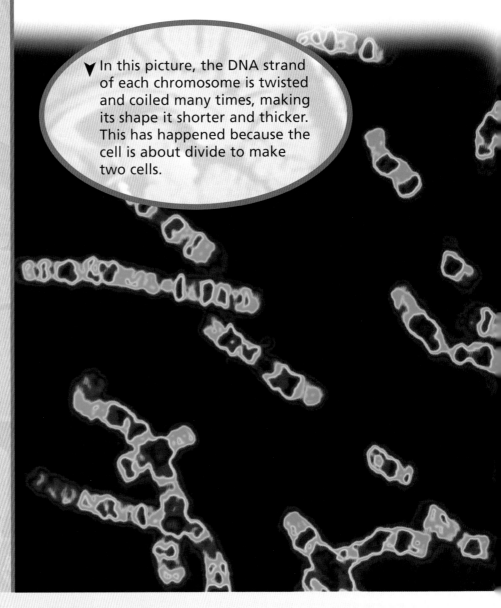

▼ In this picture, the DNA strand of each chromosome is twisted and coiled many times, making its shape it shorter and thicker. This has happened because the cell is about divide to make two cells.

chromosome thread of DNA, carrying thousands of genes
genetic to do with genes

Changing shape

Chromosomes can change shape. Usually their DNA is unravelled long and thin, like pieces of stretched-out string. These are very difficult to see under the microscope. But if the cell is about to divide, as shown later, the chromosomes change. In each one the DNA strand twists into a thicker, shorter coil, like twisting an elastic band tight.

In the control centre

The 46 chromosomes do not float about anywhere in the **cell**. They are inside the **nucleus**. The nucleus is usually a rounded blob somewhere near the middle of the cell. It contains the chromosomes, which have the genes that tell all parts of the cell what to do.

Different lengths

The chromosomes (strands of DNA) inside each cell are not all the same length. Chromosome number 1 is the longest DNA strand, with 245 million pairs of bases. Number 2 is slightly shorter, and so on. The average stretched-straight length for one chromosome is about 47 mm.

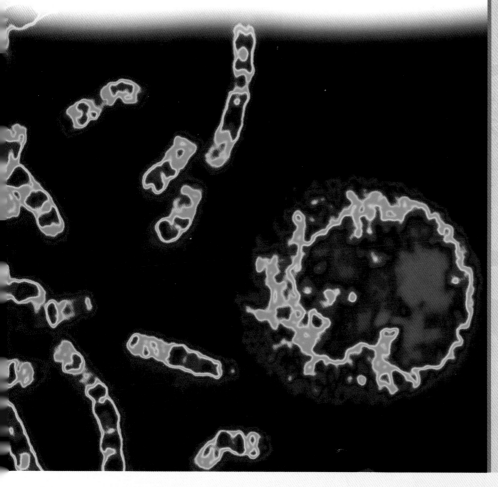

nucleus   control centre of a cell, containing DNA

What are genes?

If 1 = A, 2 = B, 3 = C and so on, what does 7 5 14 5 spell out? This is information or instructions written in code. Codes can be in many different forms, like numbers, letters, words, diagrams – and chemicals. **DNA** contains its **genetic** information in the form of a chemical code.

Twisted ladder

Each long strand of DNA in a chromosome is shaped like a ladder which has been twisted like a corkscrew. This shape is known as a **double helix**. The two long sides of the ladder are the same all the way along. But the cross-parts or "rungs" of the ladder are not. They are made of small chemical units called **bases**, joined together in pairs. There are four kinds of base. They are known by the first letters of their chemical names – A (**adenine**), T (**thymine**), C (**cytosine**), and G (**guanine**).

Junk DNA

In each cell, there is far more DNA than is needed for the body's 30,000 genes. It is like a book with many more blank pages than written ones. However the "blank pages", called junk DNA, may have useful jobs controlling and organizing the genes.

Genetic code

A **gene** is one small section of a strand of DNA. The order of the bases along this small section "spells" information. If we write them out as letters, like GACTTAGGCTAC and so on, they look pretty strange. An average gene is 3,000 bases long. That's a lot of As, Cs, Ts and Gs. It would be a very long word that looks like nonsense to us. But to the **cell**, the order of the 3,000 bases is a single gene or **genetic** instruction, telling the cell how to do something.

This is how your cells know things like what shape your features should be and what colour your hair will be – it is all written in your genetic code.

SECRET OF LIFE!

In 1953, two scientists, James Watson (left) and Francis Crick (right), worked out the mysterious, ladder-like shape of DNA. In the year 2000 Watson and Crick's work was voted one of the top three scientific discoveries of the 20th century.

bases   "rungs of the ladder" in DNA, consisting of four chemicals whose order carries genetic instructions.

Tiny, but huge!

All the lengths of DNA for the complete set of human genes have about 3,200 million "rungs" or pairs of bases. If this DNA was the size of a real ladder, it would be almost one million kilometres long; enough to go around the Earth 25 times.

◄ The "twisted ladder" of DNA contains genetic information in its "rungs", where there are pairs of bases that make up a unique code.

Making new parts

Inside a cell, such as the plasma cell below, tiny blob-shaped ribosomes are like assembly lines in factories. They follow information in the genes, to build up new proteins. The proteins are then joined together to make larger body parts.

How genes work

The plans for a house would be of little use on their own, with no one to use them. You need to make copies of the plans, and give them out to people with the skills to build each part. These people then read the plans, make the different parts shown, and fit them together to make the finished result. **Genetic** information is similar. It is also copied, read and used to make its finished results.

Reading genes

One **gene** is like one short part of the whole string of **DNA** in a **chromosome**. Genes are copied as lengths of a similar substance, **RNA**. These RNA copies are sent out of the **nucleus**, to other parts of the cell.

A body cell uses its genetic ➤ instructions to build up new substances, in the way that factory production lines assemble cars and other products.

nucleus

ribosomes

RNA   ribonucleic acid, which uses DNA instructions to build substances inside cells

Building work

In the cell, the RNA copies of the genes attach to ball-shaped parts called **ribosomes**. The ribosomes use the instructions from the genes to join together very small, simple chemical substances in the cell, to build a bigger, more complicated result. The finished result is a **protein** – a "building block" substance for the body.

Just as bricklayers or carpenters have different tasks when building a house, different genes have their own instructions for making different kinds of proteins. These various proteins make up your different body parts, like muscles, nerves, skin, and bones.

Finished product

Several genes control the colour of your eyes. They contain the instructions for making the coloured substances, called **pigments**, at the front of the eye. These special genes are only switched on in the cells of the coloured part of the eye, the iris.

ribosomes   parts in a cell where simple chemicals are joined together according to DNA instructions

Pairs of genes

Each of your body's **cells** contains two full sets of genetic instructions, as strands of **DNA** called **chromosomes**. Apart from a couple of special cells (which we will look at later), every cell has two complete sets of chromosomes, with two complete sets of genes.

From the parents

As there are two complete sets of genes in a cell, they make a pair. One set of 23 chromosones matches the other set of 23, to make 46 chromosomes in every cell.

The reason for having two sets goes back to when a human body begins its life as a single microscopic cell called the **fertilized egg**.

In pairs

The chromosomes from a single human cell are usually spread around the **nucleus**. When pictures of them are taken through a microscope, the chromosomes can be matched up into pairs, because each member of a pair looks like the other.

▲ In a sports team, each player has an opponent in the other team doing the same job. Likewise in a human body cell, there are two sets of genes, each with much the same task.

fertilized egg   the result of an egg cell joining a sperm cell, which can then divide again and again, developing into a new human body

In the egg, one of the sets of 23 chromosomes came from the mother. The other set of 23 came from the father. How this happens is shown later on.

Two genes for one

Because you have a pair of chromosomes in each cell, each gene is in a pair, too. For many genes, both members of the pair are exactly the same. They contain the same information for making the same bit of the body – such as your eye colour. But in some cases the members of the pair are slightly different. This is partly what makes you unique, as you will find on pages 18-19.

More and less

Other animals, and plants too, have pairs of chromosomes like us. But most have a different numbers of pairs, not 23. The number of pairs is not linked to the size of the animal or plant, or to its total number of genes.

Fruit fly	4 pairs
Housefly	6 pairs
Cat	19 pairs
Human	23 pairs
Horse	32 pairs
Dog	39 pairs
Pigeon	40 pairs
Goldfish	47 pairs
Crayfish	100 pairs

Dimple test

When you smile, do you have dimples in your cheeks? This depends on your genes. If both alleles of the dimple gene are "dimple", you will have them. Even if you only have one "dimple" gene, you will still get them – as the "dimple" allele is more dominant than the "no-dimple" one.

Taking over

Do your earlobes hang low, do they wobble to and fro? It depends on your **genes**. You have a double-set of genes in every body cell. So you have two genes giving instructions for every feature, like whether you have dangly earlobes or not. But these genes might not be giving exactly the same instructions.

Some genes have several different versions, known as **alleles**. You received one allele from your mother and the other from your father. Your earlobe shape (or other feature) depends on how these alleles work together. They both have the instructions to make the same part, but one may want it to be large, the other may want it to be small.

allele   version of a gene that controls how a body part is made or works

Trial of strength

If both genes for earlobes are the "dangly" alleles, you will have dangly earlobes. If both genes are "small", your earlobes will be small. But what if there is one allele for "dangly" and the other is for "small"?

The "small" earlobe allele is stronger or **dominant**, compared to the "dangly" one, which is weaker or **recessive**. So the dominant one will win, and you will have small earlobes. Many genes act in a dominant or recessive way. It makes genetics quite complicated!

Which gene is boss?

In the table, you can see that the dominant version of a gene overpowers the recessive one. The recessive result only happens if someone has two recessive versions of the gene.

GENE FOR	DOMINANT ALLELE (stronger version)	RECESSIVE ALLELE (weaker version)
Hair colour	Darker hair	Lighter hair
Hair loss (men)	Early hair loss	Late hair loss
Eyelash length	Longer eyelashes	Shorter eyelashes
Arch of foot	Up-curved arch	Flatter arch

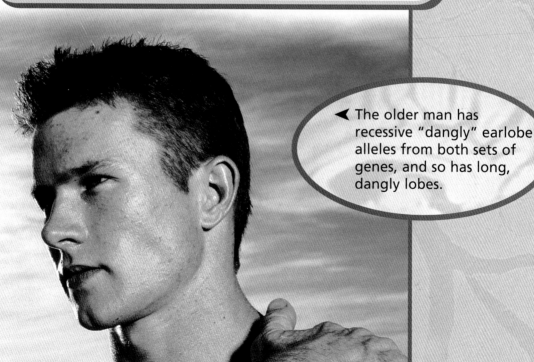

◄ The older man has recessive "dangly" earlobe alleles from both sets of genes, and so has long, dangly lobes.

New cells for old

Every second, five million tiny parts of you die. They are microscopic cells that have done their jobs and their lives have come to an end. But every second, about the same number of new cells are "born" to take their place.

The body constantly maintains, repairs and renews itself, by replacing old cells with new ones. It does this using various types of **stem cells**. These are cells which are specialized to make more cells, by dividing in half, and then growing back to full size. The process is called **cell division**.

How long do cells live?

Different kinds of cells in the body live for different amounts of time, before they are replaced by cell division. This time span is built into the genes.

TYPE OF CELL	LIFE SPAN
Cheek inner lining cell	12 hours
Stomach inner lining cell	2 days
Germ-eating white blood cell	12 days
Taste cell on tongue	30 days
Outer skin cell (epidermis)	30 days
Red blood cell	120 days
Liver cell	18 months
Bone cell	10 years
Nerve cell (below)	Same lifetime as the body

Divide and multiply

As a stem cell divides, it copies all the tiny parts inside it, including the **nucleus** and all the **DNA**, into both the new cells. Each of the two new cells then has a "choice". It can stay as a stem cell, and divide again. Or it can start to become specialized, by switching on certain genes which make it into a nerve cell, muscle cell, bone cell or another type of cell. The "choice" depends on what your body needs at that time.

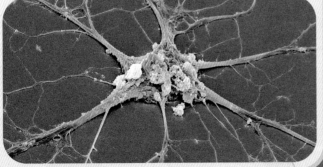

This cell is just dividing ➤ into two. Each new nucleus has the same DNA, but the two cells may end up switching on different genes to do different tasks.

Stem cells

Stem cells have the ability to become almost any kind of specialized cell. This does not work the other way round – cells which are already specialized, like muscle, bone and blood cells, cannot become stem cells. Medical scientists (below) are studying how to train stem cells to make the specialized cells that ill people need to rebuild damaged parts.

stem cells   cells which make specialized cells, such as blood or skin cells

Two sets

Before a cell divides, its 23 pairs of DNA strands, the chromosomes, copy themselves. Then the strands coil up thicker and shorter and each moves next to its partner. As splitting happens, one set of chromosome pairs moves into each resulting cell. This process is called **mitosis**.

Copy, copy, copy

When you get a new mobile phone, you need a set of instructions. **Cells** in the body are the same. Each one needs its own instructions, or **genes**. So when a cell divides, as shown on the previous page, part of this division means copying genes – in other words, copying **DNA**.

DNA unzipped

DNA is designed to copy itself. This is possible because of the pairs of **bases** that form the "rungs" of the DNA ladder, as shown earlier. On each rung, the base T always links to A, and C always links to G.

To copy itself, the strand of DNA first "unzips" by breaking the link between each pair of bases. This produces two half-ladders. Then the half ladders each build a new half, to make themselves whole again.

To copy itself, DNA splits ➤ down the middle. Each existing half builds up a new half that is an exact copy of the old one, as seen here.

DNA polymerase enzyme that enables DNA to copy itself

Two the same

If base T exists on the half ladder, the new base it needs to join up with must be A. For each G, the base which joins it has to be its partner C. Base by base, each half-ladder builds a new other half.

The result is two new ladders, or strands of DNA, for the two cells produced by cell division. Each is an exact copy of the other. This happens millions of times every second in your body, to make new cells that replace old, worn-out ones.

DNA fingerprints

DNA copies itself using a substance called **DNA polymerase**. In the laboratory, scientists can use DNA polymerase to make millions of copies of a tiny sample of DNA. They can then make a **genetic fingerprint**, which like a real fingerprint, is unique to each person.

Genetic fingerprints show up like the bar code of a product in the supermarket.

genetic fingerprint   code on a strand of DNA, unique to each person

Not exact copies

If you copy out words, sooner or later you will probably make a mistake. You might miss out a letter, or swap two words, or even leave out a whole sentence. **DNA** is similar. Usually its copying process, called **DNA replication**, is exact. But sometimes there is a mistake.

Kinds of errors

There are several kinds of copying mistakes that happen in DNA. One of the chemical units called **bases** might get broken off, or not attach itself to the right partner. Sometimes a whole section of a DNA strand gets missed out, or is copied twice.

Or part of a strand may come loose and then get added into another strand – in other words, it moves from one chromosome to another. These changes to the normal set of genes are known as **mutations**.

Causes of change

There are various causes of mutations in DNA:

✦ Certain types of the tiniest germs known as **viruses**.

✦ Some chemicals including those in certain drugs.

✦ Forms of energy known as radiation, such as ultra-violet, X-rays and gamma rays.

Radiation or **radioactivity** *is invisible, but it can seriously damage DNA in the body's cells and cause various forms of illness.*

DNA replication copying of DNA, to get two identical strands from one
mutation when DNA is not copied exactly, changes in the new DNA strands may alter the genes

Effects and problems

The effects of these changes vary. They may happen in a "junk" part of the DNA strand and cause no trouble. Even if they happen in a part of the strand which is a **gene**, they may not affect how the gene works. The effects also depend on when the changes happen – very early in life during development as a baby, or later as an adult. For example, if a DNA mistake occurs during usual body maintenance, the result may be a growth or **tumour**.

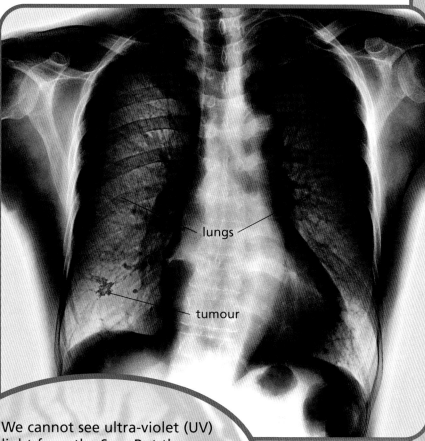

lungs

tumour

◄ We cannot see ultra-violet (UV) light from the Sun. But these rays can damage the DNA of skin cells and cause skin growths, including a form of cancer called malignant melanoma.

Passing on genes

"Aah, what a cute new baby! She's got her mother's eyes and her father's chin." Members of the same family often look alike. We say there is a family likeness or family resemblance. Some of the similarities are clear, like the colour of skin and hair. Other similarities are less obvious, like ear shape.

Many of these body features are passed on from parents to children to grandchildren, and so on, generation after generation. This is all due to the **genes**.

Missing out

Sometimes a grandparent has a body feature, the parent does not, but then the grandchild does. This usually involves the **recessive** version of a gene. We say the feature "skips a generation".

Sometimes features like red hair "skip a generation" because of the way genes work.

Family likeness is strongest between ➤ parents and children, since their genes are most similar. The resemblance gets less with more distant relations like aunts, uncles and cousins.

Body language   **generation**   different age groups in a family, like children, parents, and grandparents

Inheritance

Each person has a double set of genes, one from the mother and one from the father. Because of the way certain genes are dominant, some of a child's body features are from one parent, and some from the other. When children grow up to become mothers or fathers, they pass on a unique selection of genes to the next child. The passing on of genes is known as **inheritance**.

"You've got your Gran's nose"

If you have a feature like your grandparents, but not like your parents, this is how it happened.

+ The grandparent has two **recessive** versions of the gene, so the feature shows up.

+ The parent inherits one recessive version, but also a dominant version from the other grandparent, so the recessive feature is "overpowered".

+ The grandchild inherits recessive versions from both parents, and the feature returns.

---

inheritance   when something gets passed from parent to child due to genes

Two ones make two

For about one day, you were a single living **cell** smaller than the dot on this "i". Every human body begins as a cell like this, called the **fertilized** egg. It is made when two other cells join together – an egg cell from the mother, and a **sperm** cell from the father. Both egg cell and sperm cell contain **genes**. The mother's genes in the egg come together with the father's genes in the sperm, to make a new set – the baby's genes. This is how we **inherit** genes from our parents.

Making eggs

Egg cells are made in the female body parts called **ovaries**, as shown on page 30. As with sperm cells, each egg contains only one set of genes, not the usual two.

DIFFERENT ...
The egg cell (below) is rounded and about one-tenth of one millimetre across, which is huge compared to ordinary body cells.

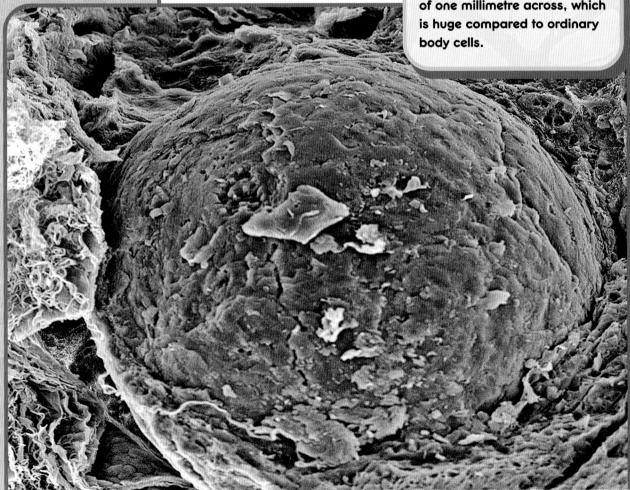

meiosis cell division that forms egg and sperm cells, where each cell gets
only one set of chromosomes, not the usual double-set

Doubling each time

But there is a catch. Both parents have a complete double-set of genes in each body cell. If the egg and sperm cells had these, then when they joined, the fertilized egg would have four sets. This does not happen, because egg and sperm cells are made by a special kind of cell division called **meiosis**.

One set only

When a cell with two complete sets of genes divides by meiosis, each resulting cell receives only one of the complete sets. This happens to egg and sperm cells. When the egg and sperm join, the two single sets come together, to make the usual double set in the fertilized egg. This can now begin normal cell division by mitosis, to start forming the baby's body.

Making sperm

Sperm cells are made in the male body parts called **testes**, as shown on page 32. Each sperm contains only one set of genes, not the usual two as in other body cells.

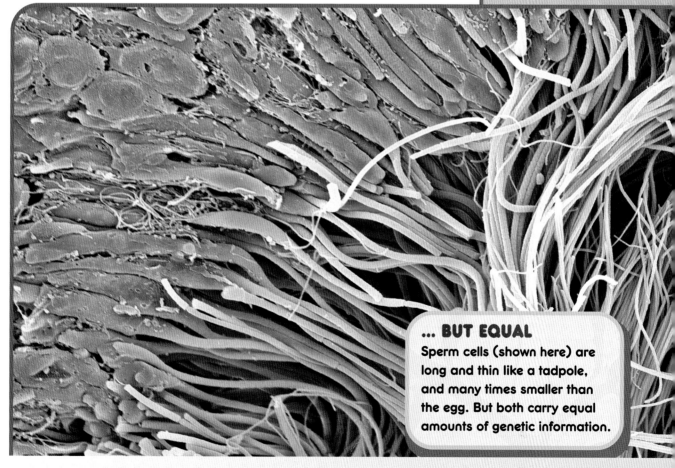

... BUT EQUAL
Sperm cells (shown here) are long and thin like a tadpole, and many times smaller than the egg. But both carry equal amounts of genetic information.

Female reproductive parts

One of the first questions about you when you were born was "is it a boy or a girl?" Male and female bodies have mostly the same parts, like skin, muscles, heart, lungs and stomach. But some important parts are not the same. These are called the reproductive parts, because they are used for **reproduction** – making babies.

Egg release

In the female reproductive parts, the egg cells are formed in two rounded **ovaries**. Every 28 days or so, one egg cell becomes bigger and ripe, and breaks out of the ovary's surface. It moves slowly along a tube called the **oviduct**, towards the **womb**, a journey that takes four or five days.

Female parts

The female reproductive parts are all inside the lower **abdomen** (unlike the male ones). They begin to develop during puberty, which usually begins at the age of 10-13 years.

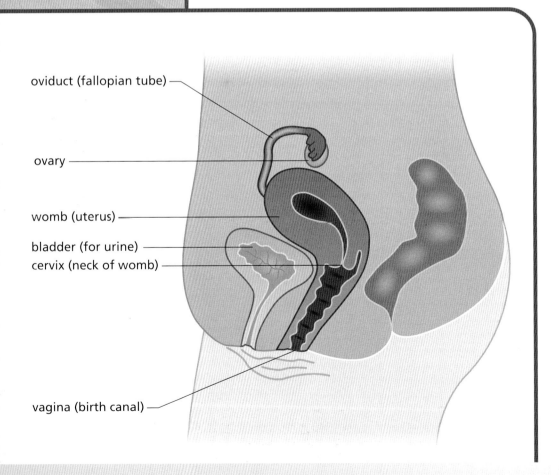

oviduct (fallopian tube)

ovary

womb (uterus)

bladder (for urine)

cervix (neck of womb)

vagina (birth canal)

abdomen lower part of the body or torso
puberty when sexual or reproductive parts begin to work

The female cycle

Over the seven to ten days before the ripe egg is released, the inner lining of the womb has become thick with many tiny **blood vessels**. It is making itself ready to nourish the egg if it gets fertilized.

If there is no fertilized egg, the womb lining breaks into pieces. It passes along the **vagina** (birth canal) and out of the body as bleeding called a period or **menstruation**. Then the whole process of releasing a ripe egg begins again.

This whole process is called the menstrual cycle, and it is controlled by natural "messenger" substances in the body. These are **hormones**, mainly oestrogen and progesterone.

Egg cell numbers

+ By the time a baby girl is born, up to half a million egg cells have already been made in her ovaries.

+ This number is about 200,000 by the time of puberty, due to natural wearing out of cells.

+ During the fertile years, when a woman can have babies, about 400 eggs become ripe and are released, one after the other, with each menstrual cycle.

◄ The reproductive parts of the body are the only ones that do not work during childhood. They begin to do so in **puberty**.

Male reproductive parts

In the male reproductive parts, sperm cells are formed in two rounded **testes**, also known as **testicles**. Unlike egg cells, which are released every 28 days, sperm cells are made all the time, thousands every second. They begin as microscopic blobs in about 800 tiny narrow tubes called **seminiferous tubules**, tightly coiled within each testis. Over several weeks the sperm cells change shape, becoming long and thin, with a rounded head and long, bendy tail.

Ready to leave

When sperm cells are fully formed, they are stored in another coiled tube next to the testis, the **epididymis**. To leave the body and join an egg cell, they pass from here along a curving tube, the **sperm duct**.

Male parts

The main male reproductive parts are below the lower abdomen. Every day millions of sperm are formed. If they do not leave during ejaculation, they harmlessly break apart and the leftovers are taken back into the body.

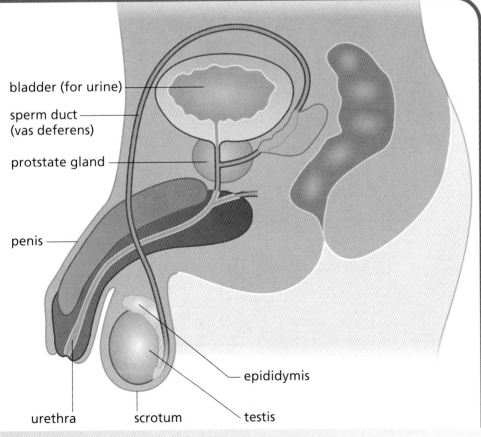

- bladder (for urine)
- sperm duct (vas deferens)
- protstate gland
- penis
- urethra
- scrotum
- epididymis
- testis

ejaculation   muscle-powered action that pushes sperm through the sperm duct and urethra, and out of the end of the penis

The sperm ducts from the two testes join inside a part known as the **prostate gland**. This adds fluid to the sperm, to give them energy so they can swish their tails and swim along.

The final journey

The sperm in their fluid then pass along a final tube, the **urethra**. This is inside another male part, the **penis**. The urethra carries the sperm to the outside by the muscle-powered action of **ejaculation**. Making sperm cells is controlled by **hormones**. The main male hormone is testosterone.

◄ From about 10-13 years old, the bodies of girls and boys become more different, mainly as the result of the hormones made by their reproductive parts.

prostate gland   male part which adds fluid to sperm cells as they are released
seminiferous tubules   coiled tubes in the testis where sperm cells are made

Getting together

Egg and sperm cells carry only one set of genes. For a human body to develop, it needs the normal double set in each cell. This is formed when an egg cell and **sperm** cell come together, usually in the egg tube (**oviduct**) of the mother. The egg cell has travelled from the nearby **ovary**, probably only a thumb's length away. The sperm cells have a much longer journey, almost half a metre.

One only

After one sperm cell has joined the egg cell at fertilization, the egg develops a hard outer layer to keep away other sperm cells. Otherwise it would receive too many sets of genes and could not develop properly.

If one of the sperm cells enters ➤ the egg cell, at **conception**, a new combination of genes is formed, from a selection of the mother's and father's genes.

conception   when an egg cell and sperm cell join to form a fertilized egg

Long journey

During **ejaculation**, the sperm cells pass out of the father's body. If this happens during **sexual intercourse**, the male **penis** is inside the female **vagina**, so the sperm cells can swim into the womb, through it, and out along the two oviducts.

Millions of sperm cells die on this huge journey, and many go into the wrong oviduct where there is no egg.

Genes come together

Finally some sperm cells reach the egg cell. One of them pushes up against it, and its head end joins with the outer layer of the egg cell. The 23 **chromosomes** inside the sperm cell's head, each one a strand of **DNA**, pass to the inside of the egg cell. Here they meet the 23 DNA strands of the egg cell. The father's genes and mother's genes have come together as a new, unique double set, ready to control the development of the new baby.

GENETIC COUNSELLING

Illnesses and problems caused by faulty genes are called genetic conditions. People with a family history of a **genetic condition** that makes life difficult for them can receive help from an expert, a genetic counsellor. The counsellor advises on the risk of it being passed on to their children.

Medical help

Sometimes a woman and man cannot have a baby in the usual way, by sexual intercourse. Eggs taken from the woman's body can be mixed in a dish with sperm from the man. After fertilization in the dish, the developing egg is put into the woman's womb, to grow. This type of **infertility** treatment is known as IVF, "in vitro fertilization", or the "test-tube baby" method.

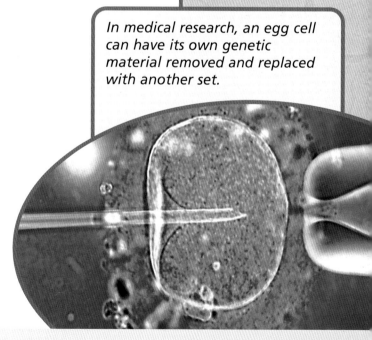

In medical research, an egg cell can have its own genetic material removed and replaced with another set.

New baby

Every new human body starts as a single dot-sized **cell**, the **fertilized egg** – but not for long. After a few hours it starts to divide by the normal method, copying all its **genes** first so each resulting cell has the full double set. A few hours later the same happens, and so on. After a few days there is a ball-like shape of several hundred cells. This nests into the thick lining of the **womb**, takes in nourishment, and continues to grow.

Girl or boy?

Genes tell the new baby to develop as a girl or boy. This happens because of two **chromosomes** called sex chromosomes. They are the 23rd of the 23 pairs of chromosomes.

The other 22 pairs of chromosomes have numbers, like pair 1, pair 2, and so on. The 23rd pair of sex chromsomes are called by letters, X and Y. In the cells of a man this pair is one large X chromosome and a smaller Y chromosome. In the cells of a woman they are both the same, X and X.

More than one baby

Sometimes two or more egg cells are released during the female cycle, and are fertilized by sperm cells. So two or more babies grow at the same time in the womb. Two are twins, three are triplets, and four are quads. They can be all boys, all girls, or a mixture. Their genes are as similar to each other as those of any brothers and sisters.

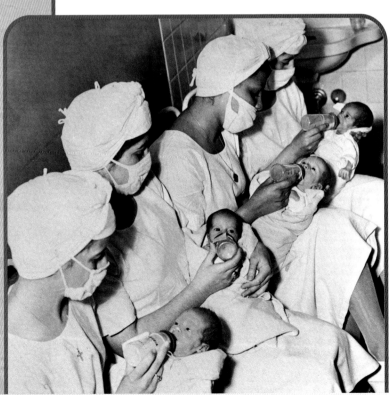

X and Y

As egg cells form in a woman, each always gets one X chromosome. When a **sperm** cell forms in a man, it can receive either an X or a Y. When an egg and sperm join, the two sex chromosomes get together. The Y chromosome contains the genes to make a male baby, and these are more **dominant** than the X genes for a female baby.

So, if an X-carrying sperm cell joins an X-containing egg cell, the result is XX, and a baby girl will develop. But if the sperm cell has a Y, the result is XY, so the developing baby will be a boy.

ARE YOU XX OR XY?

Y is more dominant than X in the sex chromosomes, so a Y chromosome from the father means the baby will be a boy.

Mother's chromosome	Father's chromosome	Baby's sex
X	X	female
X	Y	male

Identical twins

Sometimes one fertilized egg divides into two cells, then these separate and each continues to develop into a baby. The result is identical twins. They have exactly the same genes and look very similar indeed when babies.

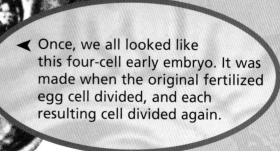

◄ Once, we all looked like this four-cell early embryo. It was made when the original fertilized egg cell divided, and each resulting cell divided again.

Life in the womb

The start of a human body is a very busy time for **genes**. The **cells** are dividing fast, moving about and becoming specialized as their various groups of genes switch on. They shape body parts like the brain, heart, muscles and skin. For the first eight weeks after **fertilization**, the developing baby is called an **embryo**. At the end of this time it is smaller than a thumb. Yet all its main body parts are formed, even its little fingers and toes, according to the **genetic** instructions.

Pregnancy

From eight weeks until birth, the developing baby is called a **fetus**. It grows a lot, and its body parts become bigger and stronger. Genetic instructions continue to work as finishing touches are added to its body, such as fingernails and toenails.

The whole time of growth in the womb is called pregnancy, and lasts about nine months.

Warm and dark

The baby floats in a pool of fluid inside its mother's **womb**. It doesn't breathe air or eat food. It gets all it needs from its mother, through the **placenta**. This also forms according to genetic instructions.

About four weeks after ➤ fertilization, the baby does not yet look like a human, as its face, arms, legs, and other parts have not formed.

placenta   part in the wall of the womb which passes oxygen and nourishment from mother to baby

First check-up

During pregnancy, the mother usually has an **ultrasound scan** to see the baby inside. This gives early warning if the baby is not developing properly, perhaps because of a problem in its genes.

A gene problem could be passed on from its parents, as an **inherited** condition. Or it could be a new problem that has cropped up in the baby's own genes, as a result of a **mutation**.

About eight weeks after ▼ fertilization, the baby begins to look like a tiny human being, as it passes from the embryo to the fetus stage.

Ultrasound scan

One or two scans are usually taken between 10 and 28 weeks after the start of pregnancy. Very high-pitched sound waves beam into the womb and bounce back off the baby's body parts. These echoes are combined by computer to show a picture of the baby on a screen.

Some mothers wish to give birth in hospital, where medical help is at hand. Others prefer the familiar quiet sounds of home.

---

ultrasound scan   image of the inside of the body (to see a baby in the womb) made using sounds which are too high for humans to hear

It's your birthday!

After nine months the baby is ready to leave the **womb** at birth. Its **genes** have guided its growth and development from a single fertilized egg **cell**, into a body made of millions of millions of cells, often weighing more than three kilograms. The original dot-sized egg cell has increased in size 10 billion times!

Leaving the womb

After the wet, dark, quiet, cramped warmth of the womb, the baby comes into brighter, cooler, noisier, drier outside world. It begins to breathe for itself, usually opening up its airways by crying loudly! It also feeds for itself, usually from its mother's milk. Its life may seem to be just beginning, but its unique set of genes has already been together for months.

Lots of babies

Around the world, new sets of genes are being made every three seconds – this is how often a new baby is born.

After four to six months, the fetus starts to stretch, kick, and suck its thumb.

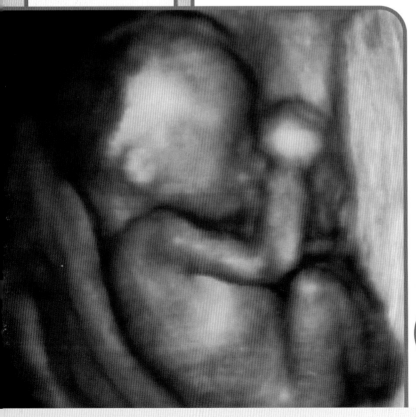

The minutes and hours ➤ after birth are very precious, as the baby and mother rest and get to know each other.

Genetic problems

Rarely, birth shows that the new baby has a **genetic** problem. This might be the way its body has developed. For example, it might have one finger less or one too many, or a cleft palate – a gap in the roof of its mouth. Usually doctors carry out operations as soon as possible, to treat the problem.

Other genetic problems may not show up until later, perhaps affecting the baby's heart or the way its brain works.

"We knew there was a risk that Emma might have Fragile X, but she has grown up fine."

Marla, whose family have a history of Fragile X Syndrome. In this genetic condition there is a faulty gene, FMR1, on the X sex chromosome. It affects the brain's intelligence, memory and learning abilities.

Too many chromosomes

Down's syndrome is a genetic condition caused by having three copies of **chromosome** number 21 in each body cell, instead of the usual two. It has various effects on appearance and how the brain works. Yet many people with the condition (like the boy in the centre here) make great personal achievements.

Not "all in the genes"

As we grow up, **genes** have many effects on our lives. They shape features like skin colour, hair type, and our height as an adult. We cannot alter our genes, although medical scientists are trying to develop new treatments. This is called **gene therapy**, and it is being done to treat various **inherited** and **genetic** conditions.

Different conditions

Imagine shiny new cars rolling off the production line. They all start out much the same. But after several years, they are different, depending on the care their owners take. Some of the cars might be serviced and cleaned often, still look good and run well. Others suffer neglect, breakdowns and accidents, and look dirty and damaged. A few are already in the scrap yard.

gene therapy   treating a medical condition by altering or replacing faulty genes

Taking care

Like the cars, our bodies respond to the care of their owners – us! This includes the food we eat, our activities and sports, how we behave, our relationships with family and friends, the likes and dislikes we develop, how hard we try at school, and many other aspects of daily life.

Your genes have a lot of say in what you will become. But so do your surroundings and environment. And, as you get older, so do the choices you make for yourself.

Gene therapy

Medical research is trying to find ways of changing faulty genes. Gene therapy has been tried, to replace faulty cells with normal cells, so they will multiply and take over. Results so far are mixed, but gene therapy is a great hope for the future.

◄ Our genes have many effects, especially on the appearance of our bodies, but so do our personal choices and behaviour.

Find out more

Where to search

Search engine

A search engine looks through the entire web and lists all sites that match the words in the search box. It can give thousands of links, but the best matches are at the top of the list, on the first page. Try bbc.co.uk/search

Search directory

A search directory is like a library of websites that have been sorted by a person instead of a computer. You can search by keyword or subject and browse through the different sites like you look through books on a library shelf. A good example is yahooligans.com

Books

The Reproductive System, Steve Parker (Heinemann Library, 2003)

Genes and DNA, Richard Walker (Kingfisher, 2003)

Genetics, Robert Sneddon (Franklin Watts, 2004)

World Wide Web

If you want to find out more about genes and reproduction, you can search the Internet using keywords like these:

- 'identical twins' - sperm + egg - double helix

You can also find your own keywords by using headings or words from this book. Use the search tips below to help you find the most useful websites.

Search tips

There are billions of pages on the Internet so it can be difficult to find exactly what you are looking for. These search skills will help you find useful websites more quickly:

Use simple keywords instead of whole sentences

- Use two to six keywords in a search, putting the most important words first
- Be precise – use names of people, places or things
- If you want to find words that go together, put quote marks around them, for example 'stomach acid'
- Use the advanced section of your search engine
- Use the + sign between keywords to link them, for example typing + KS3 after your keyword will help you find web pages at the right level.

Glossary

abdomen lower part of the body or torso

adenine one of the four chemical units called bases in DNA, which is like a letter in the genetic code, and carries genetic information

allele version of a gene which controls how a certain body part is made or works

bases "rungs of the ladder" in DNA, consisting of four chemicals whose order carries genetic instructions

blood vessels arteries, capillaries and veins – tubes through which blood flows

carcinogens substances that trigger cancerous growths or tumours

cell division when one cell splits to make two cells

cells microscopic "building blocks" which make up all body parts

chromosome thread of DNA, carrying thousands of genes

conception when an egg cell and sperm cell join to form a fertilized egg

cytosine one of the four chemical units called bases in DNA, like a letter in the genetic code, carrying genetic information

DNA De-oxyribonucleic acid, which contains the genes

DNA polymerase enzyme that enables DNA to copy itself

DNA replication copying DNA to get two identical strands from one

dominant when one version of a gene is stronger than another (which is called recessive), so its genetic instructions are followed

double helix the shape of the chemical DNA

ejaculation muscle-powered action that pushes sperm from the sperm duct out of the penis

embryo developing baby from fertilization to eight weeks old

epididymis coiled tube in the testis where sperm are stored

fallopian tube another name for the oviduct tube from the ovary to the womb

fertilized egg the result of an egg cell joining a sperm cell, which can then divide again and again, developing into a new human body

fetus developing baby in the womb, from eight weeks old until birth

gene therapy treating a medical condition by altering or replacing faulty genes

generation different age groups in a family, like children, parents, and grandparents

genes instructions for how the body grows, develops and works

genetic condition medical problem due to a fault in the genes

genetic fingerprint code on a strand of DNA, unique to each person

genetic to do with genes

guanine one of the four chemical units called bases in DNA, like a letter in the genetic code, carrying genetic information

hormones substances made by hormonal or endocrine glands, which spread around the body in the blood and affect or control the way that various parts work

human genome complete set of genes for the human body

infertility when a man and woman have difficulty in conceiving a baby

inheritance when something gets passed from parent to child due to genes

malignant when growths or tumours spread to other body parts, as in many types of cancer

meiosis cell division that forms egg and sperm cells, where each cell only gets one set of chromosomes, not the usual double-set

menstruation when the womb lining passes out along the vagina, as the bleeding called a period

mitosis type of cell division where each of the two new cells gets a full double set of chromosomes (two sets of all the genes)

mutation when DNA is not copied exactly, so changes in the new DNA strands may alter the genes

nerves string-like parts that carry messages around the body as tiny pulses of electricity

nucleus control centre of a cell, containing DNA

ovaries two female body parts that make egg cells and hormones called oestrogen and progesterone

oviduct tube from the ovary to the womb in the female body, also known as the fallopian tube

oxygen gas which makes up one-fifth of air, and which the body needs

penis male body part through which sperm are released and urine passes from the bladder

pigment substance with a particular colour in paints, or in skin, hair, and the eye

placenta part in the womb wall which passes oxygen and nourishment from mother to baby

prostate gland part in the male body which adds fluid to sperm cells as they are released

proteins substances, in the body and from foods, which are used mainly for building and growing

puberty when sexual or reproductive parts begin to work

radioactivity energy waves from atoms breaking up, which can cause harm to living things

recessive when one version of a gene is weaker than another (which is called dominant), so its genetic instructions are not followed

red blood cells cells specialized to carry oxygen around the body

reproduction breeding, when living things make more of their kind – in humans, having a baby

ribosomes parts within a cell, where simple chemical substances are joined together according to DNA instructions

RNA ribonucleic acid, which uses genetic instructions from DNA to build substances inside cells

seminiferous tubules coiled tubes in the testis, where sperm cells are made

sexual intercourse when a woman and man get together and the man's penis is inside the woman's vagina, able to release sperm cells there

sperm cell cell made by the male body, which joins with a female's egg cell to become a fertilized egg

sperm duct tube in the male body through which sperm cells are released from the testis to the penis

stem cells cells which make specialized cells such as blood or skin cells

testes two parts below the lower male body which make sperm cells and a hormone called testosterone

testicles another name for the testes

thymine one of the four chemical units called bases in DNA, like a letter in the genetic code, carrying genetic information

tumour unnatural lump or growth, usually cause by cells multiplying too fast and out of control

ultrasound scan image of inside of the body (to see a baby in the womb) made using sounds which are too high for humans to hear

urethra tube that carries the urine from the bladder out of the body

uterus female body part where a baby develops, also called the womb

vagina passageway from the womb to the outside, also called the birth canal

viruses tiniest germs, which can cause serious disease

womb female body part, also called the uterus, where a baby develops

Index